Emeralds

Are a Girl's Best Friend

Emeralds
Are a Girl's Best Friend

SUE HEADY

Introduction by
Michael O'Donoghue

CHARTWELL
BOOKS, INC.

This edition published in 1999 by
CHARTWELL BOOKS, INC.
A division of BOOK SALES, INC
114 Northfield Avenue,
Edison, New Jersey 08837

Produced by
PRC Publishing Ltd,
Kiln House, 210 New Kings Road,
London SW6 4NZ

ISBN 0 78581 098 6

Printed and bound in Hong Kong

Contents

INTRODUCTION

Emerald and ruby are the only two classic gemstones whose color does not need further description. Less rare than ruby, emerald is particularly interesting since, alone of the major species, it can disclose its place of origin to the investigative gemmologist. While this is not invariably possible, the finest stones; from Colombia, those from Russia, and from Zimbabwe, can be identified by the tiny fragments of other minerals that they include and which can be seen at around 40x magnification.

The finest emeralds are an even, soft green: the best and largest are from Colombia so it is lucky that they can readily be identified. Colombian emeralds are found in rocks that are not too hard to work and fine hexagonal crystals can be retrieved more or less unfractured. If these are not transparent enough to facet, the crystals can be sold as specimens in themselves, although this does not often happen. Mining the emeralds is something of a hit-or-miss operation and can sometimes get out of hand when a good strike of emerald is rumored.

The major Colombian mining districts are generally known as Chivor and Muzo, though each area has many small mines operating within it. Crystals are usually brought to Bogota, the capital city, for grading, faceting, and selling, but excep-

UCTION

tional stones may be cut in the USA or Germany.

Stones of equally fine color are also found in Pakistan and Afghanistan, though they do not reach such large sizes. The emeralds are located at some altitude and mining is family-based; large-scale production methods being ruled out because of geological difficulties and the relatively small yield of emerald. Very fine stones are also found in the southeast of Zimbabwe, where they are called Sandawana emeralds. Here, finds of gemstones were reported and worked for the first time as recently as the 1950s. A most useful feature of Sandawana stones is that they keep their color even down to the smallest sizes.

Emeralds from the Ural Mountains of Russia can also be well colored and of jewelry size. Stones from Transvaal, South Africa, and from India are generally, though not invariably, slightly less fine a

green, though Indian emeralds found in old oriental jewelry
are of good color and large
enough for stones to be
engraved. Small deposits of emerald
are found in a number of other
countries: for example, many of lower-
grade emeralds found in jewelry
originate in Brazil.

Today, almost all emeralds
are oiled: a light, colorless min-
eral oil is introduced through
surface-reaching cracks. The oil
"fills" hollow inclusions inside the
stone and this minimizes the scattering of
light from them and makes the stone
appear to have a greater clarity than is, in
fact, the case. Sometimes, glassy or poly-
mer material is introduced into cracks in
the same way and for the same purpose.
Oiled stones feel and smell oily — a
much-discussed topic of today is whether
or not the seller should disclose known
cases of oiling or filling to the customer. At
the time of writing, this question has not
been resolved.

Emerald can be
made in the laboratory in
sizes large enough to be faceted
and set in jewelry, although the
growth period may last up to one year for

a single carat stone.
During this process, the
rate of cooling from the melt,
controlled by computer, is critical, and
expensive in terms of staff time. This is
why synthetic emeralds are surprisingly
costly. Fortunately, the pattern
of inclusions inside natural and
synthetic emeralds is quite
distinctive and recogniz-
able to the gemmologist.

RINGS

Rings have been worn in Eastern and Western cultures, by both men and women, since they were first introduced in the third millennium BC.

These two rings are a clear indicator that it is not just the carat (or weight) which determines the price of an emerald — the color, clarity, and cut of the stone are also important. So while the ring on this page, which is made from platinum and is set with a cabochon emerald weighing 4.48 carats in a pavé-set and baguette-cut diamond tiered surround, was given an estimate by Christie's of $13,000-20,000, the cluster ring opposite, which features a cabochon emerald weighing 17.33 carats in a circular-cut diamond two-tiered surround, entered the very same sale with an estimate of $5,000-7,000.

The fact that the latter was signed by the famous jeweler Harry Winston, known as the "King of Diamonds" in the 1950s, did not increase its value further.

In 1920, at the age of just 24, Winston opened the Premier Diamond Company in New York City. He established another company under his own name 12 years later, and was soon

cutting such famous diamonds as the "Jonker," the "Taylor-Burton," the "Star of Sierra Leone," and the "Vargas." Over the years, he owned as many as one third of all the famous diamonds in the world, three of which — the "Hope," the "Portuguese," and the "Oppenheimer" — he donated to the Smithsonian. These days, the Harry Winston empire is run by his son, Ronald, who took over as president and CEO of the company on his father's death in 1978. He continues to offer "Rare Jewels of the World," the firm's motto for many years.

Estimate:
$13,000-20,000/$5,000-7,000;
Magnificent Jewels, Geneva, May 27, 1993

The cabochon emerald in this ring has been carved with hearts and weighs 34.40 carats. It is supported by tiny baguette-cut, pavé-set diamond shoulders, and a mount that is signed T & H M, which probably stands for Trabert & Hoeffer, Inc-Mauboussin. The term cabochon comes from the French word for a doorknob, *caboche*, and refers to the smooth, rounded, and highly polished surface of the emerald. This type of cut was used centuries ago, before the development of faceting (the cutting of a gemstone), and was only revived during the Art Nouveau era (1890s-early 1900s). Trabert & Hoeffer, an American jewelry firm, was founded in the 1930s by Howard Hoeffer and quickly formed an association with the French firm Mauboussin, which was already more than a century old, having been established in 1827. Together, they created a very successful line of jewelry called "Reflection," which was unique in that it combined 18 carat gold settings and a casting technique that allowed more versatile pieces of jewelry to be made.

Estimate: $13,000-15,000; *Magnificent Jewels, Geneva, May 16, 1991*

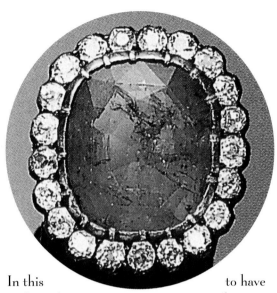

In this antique ring, a cushion-cut emerald measuring approximately 19 x 17.5 x 9.7 mm is surrounded by old mine-cut diamonds, within a gold and silver openwork mount. It is of interest primarily because it was the property of Mary Gindhart Roebling, an American woman of many firsts. In 1937, she became the first woman to serve as president and board chairman of a major American bank, when she was elected president of the Trenton Trust company. She was also the first woman governor of the American Stock Exchange (1958-59); the first living woman to have a major government building named after her — the Commerce Building in Trenton, New Jersey became the Mary G. Roebling Building; and the first female civilian aide to the Secretary of the Army. However, her name may also be familiar because it was her family who built New York City's Brooklyn Bridge.

Estimate: $10,000-12,000; *Magnificent Jewels, New York, October 24, 1995*

BRACELETS
BRACELETS

Bracelets have been worn by both men and women from very early times and in primitive, as well as civilized, societies. They lost popularity during the Middle Ages and the Renaissance, due to the long sleeves that were then fashionable, but they have enjoyed something of a revival since the 18th and 19th centuries.

These unusual looking bracelets were created by Pierre Sterlé, whose work is regarded as very typical of 1950s and 1960s jewelry design. He designed the bracelet on the left in 1950, and when the Marquise Josephina de Amodio and Moya saw it on the arm of its owner, she immediately commissioned Sterlé to produce a similar version for herself. This he did, in 1955. The "original" bracelet consists of a gold, twin-row rope bracelet with an emerald drop, a cabochon emerald, and a series of gold rope and calibré-cut emerald tassels, plus a finer gold rope and pavé-set diamond detail. The "copy" focuses on a vari-cut emerald cluster, from which a series of gold rope tassels and an emerald drop are suspended, and has a tapered gold bracelet of rope and scroll motif, which is much thicker than the earlier piece.

In general, Sterlé's work is instantly recognizable, as his ideas were original and audacious. However, despite a very loyal and wealthy international clientele, he suffered some serious financial setbacks and was forced to sell many of his designs to the leading French jewelry house of Chaumet in 1961; 15 years later, he became Chaumet's creative adviser.

Estimate: "original" $12,500-17,000; "copy" $12,500-17,000; *Magnificent Jewels,* *Geneva,* *May 18,* *1995*

The Art Deco style was launched in Paris in 1925 through the *Exposition Internationale des Art Decoratifs*, which gave the movement its name. With its abstract designs and geometric patterns, Art Deco was a direct challenge to the floral, free-flowing work of the earlier Art Nouveau era. One of the exhibitors at the *Exposition Internationale des Art Decoratifs* was the firm of Lacloche Frères, which designed this attractive Art Deco diamond and emerald bracelet around the time of the fair. Originally Spanish, Lacloche Frères was founded in Madrid in 1875 by four brothers, Fernand, Jules, Leopold, and Jacques. They subsequently opened branches in San Sebastian, Biarritz, Paris, and London. Highly successful during the 1920s and 1930s, they were known for their jewelry and *objets d'art* decorated with enamels and carved gemstones. Christie's describes this particular bracelet as an

"articulated pavé-set diamond navette-link band with calibré-cut emerald spacers, mounted in platinum." By way of explanation, pavé-set refers to the setting, which could be likened to paving stones in that many small gemstones are set very close together so as to cover the entire piece and conceal the metal base. In order that the gems fit together snugly, calibré-cut diamonds, which are small and oblong or elliptical in shape, are used. A navette is the same shape as a marquise diamond; in other words, it is boat-shaped, being elliptical and pointed at both ends.

Estimate: $43,000-52,000; *Important Jewels, San Moritz, February 23/4, 1996*

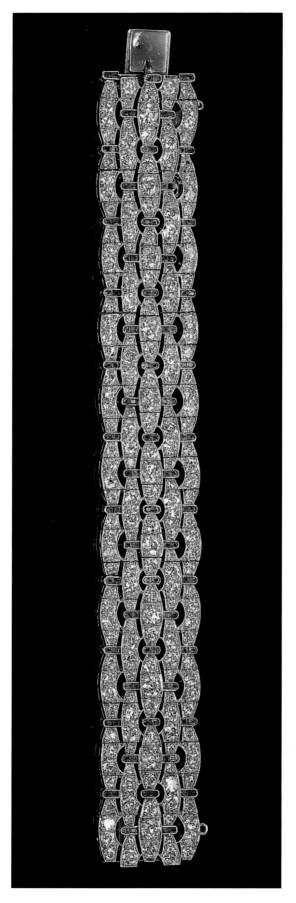

The emerald in the clasp of this bracelet is believed to have quite a history. It was first auctioned by the London branch of Christie's in June 1961, when the description in the catalog stated that "the emerald was believed to have been brought to England from India in 1760 by Robert, Lord Clive, who was nephew and ward of an ancestor of the 1961 vendor. Lord Clive is best known for his participation in the French-English Colonial Wars of 1754-1763. A member of the East India Company, he took advantage of rivalries between Indian Princes to recapture Calcutta from the French for the English."
Since then, however, the emerald, which is a cut-cornered, square-cut emerald weighing 7.01 carats, has been set in this bracelet by Boucheron, along with a three-row band of circular and marquise-cut diamonds interspersed with diamond and vari-cut emerald clusters. Boucheron was founded at the Palais Royale in 1858 by Frédéric Boucheron, who soon acquired a reputation as a precious stones expert, a masterful technician, and a creator of beautiful jewelry designs. The company remains in family hands to the present day.

Estimate:
$200,000-240,000;
*Magnificent Jewels,
Geneva, November 21,
1996*

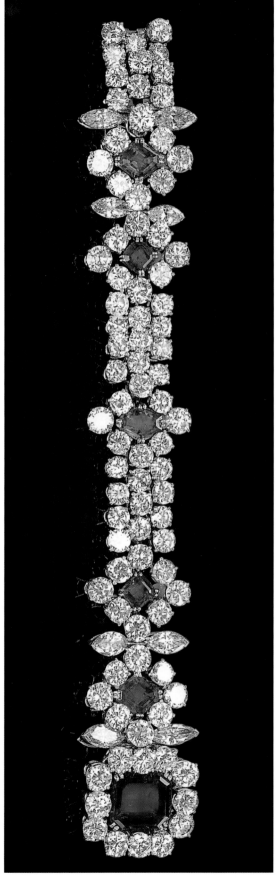

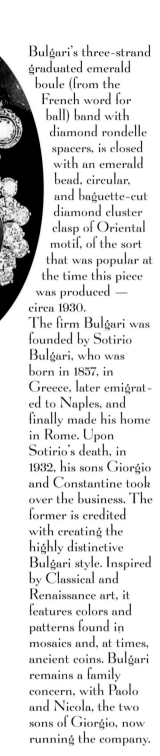

Bulgari's three-strand graduated emerald boule (from the French word for ball) band with diamond rondelle spacers, is closed with an emerald bead, circular, and baguette-cut diamond cluster clasp of Oriental motif, of the sort that was popular at the time this piece was produced — circa 1930.

The firm Bulgari was founded by Sotirio Bulgari, who was born in 1857, in Greece, later emigrated to Naples, and finally made his home in Rome. Upon Sotirio's death, in 1932, his sons Giorgio and Constantine took over the business. The former is credited with creating the highly distinctive Bulgari style. Inspired by Classical and Renaissance art, it features colors and patterns found in mosaics and, at times, ancient coins. Bulgari remains a family concern, with Paolo and Nicola, the two sons of Giorgio, now running the company.

Estimate: $15,000-20,000; *Magnificent Jewels, Geneva, November 21, 1996*

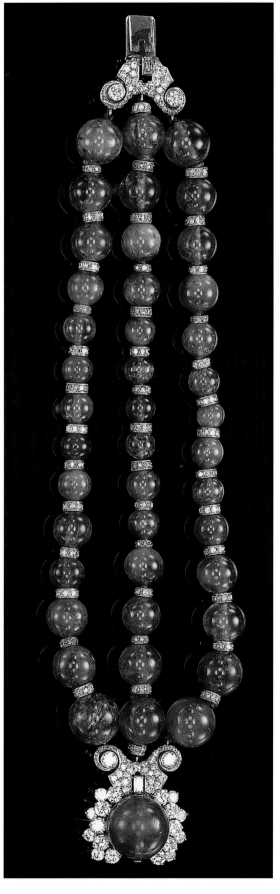

NECKLACES
NECKLACES

Necklaces, worn throughout the ages, come in all shapes and sizes. Closely fitting necklaces are usually referred to as chokers, while long, free-flowing ones are known as neck chains or sautoirs. While some are heavily laden with gems, others may be more simple with a pendant.

Pendants became popular around 1850, when they were worn either on chains or velvet bands. Cruciform pendants, such as this one, were usually made in a Latin cross or a cross with four arms of equal length and were decorated with engravings or set with gemstones. This pendant of platinum and 18 carat gold is studded with emeralds, diamonds, and cultured pearls. The cushion-shaped diamond center weighs 5.53 carats. (A cushion-shaped diamond is cut into a square or rectangular shape with rounded corners.) The other diamonds are poetically called rose-cut, which means that they have been cut in a symmetrical form, with the facets being of various shapes and

relative sizes, but characteristically having a flat base and two horizontal rows of facets rising to a point. This style, which was developed by Dutch lapidaries in the mid-17th century, lost popularity in the 18th, but once again found favor in the early part of this century.

Estimate: $110,000-135,000; *Magnificent Jewels, Geneva, May 18, 1995*

EMERALDS

This Art Deco emerald and diamond necklace was created by Cartier, one of France's leading jewelry firms. Made in 1930, it has a central pendant clip with a rectangular, cut-cornered, emerald designed as a stylized wing motif that is detachable. The panel chain has alternate links of a wing and three-stone panel. The lotus flower, which is very highly stylized to suit the geometric Art Deco elements in the necklace, is typically Egyptian and was one of Cartier's favorite decorative devices during this period. The geometry is offset by the impression of ribbon-like movement through the necklace, which has been achieved using different cuts of stone and skilled craftsmanship. Egyptian themes were a part of Cartier's repertoire from its conception in 1847 by Louis-Francois Cartier, but the passion for Egyptian artifacts in the 1920s allowed the company to further explore and adapt these exotic motifs which were to remain popular for many years. Overall, the necklace's design shows a clever synthesis of Egyptian elements and Art Deco style.

Estimate: £150,000-180,000; *Magnificent Jewels, London, June 20, 1990*

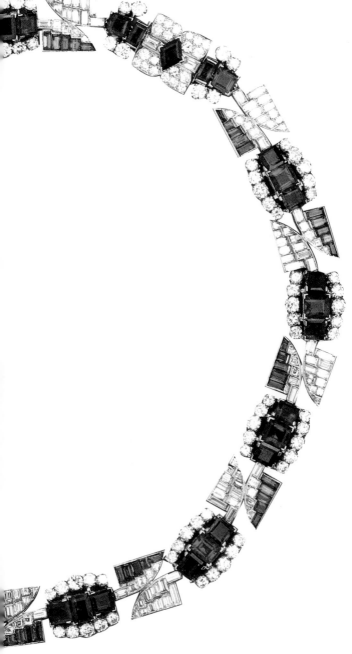

This Art Deco emerald and diamond necklace, which has been dated to circa 1930, also shows the synthesis of Egyptian elements and Art Deco style. It is signed by Cartier, London, and was sold in its original fitted leather case. The lotus flower features in the shape of the pavé-set diamond stylized mounts attached to the central rectangular emerald, from which is suspended a circular and baguette-cut diamond and an emerald bead detachable drop. The chain is made from a series of graduated, carved, cylindrical emerald beads interspersed with diamond rondelles.

Estimate: £15,000-20,000; *Important Jewellery, London, December 13, 1989*

This
delicate
Belle Epoque
emerald and dia-
mond lavaliere mea-
sures 40.5 cm long. A
lavalière, also known
as a lavalier or laval-
lière, is a type of chain
worn around a
woman's neck that
normally has one or
more gemstones
suspended from it. It
probably takes its
name from Louise
de la Vallière
(1644-1710), one of
Louis XIV's

mistresses,
who often wore chains
similar to this one.
The piece, which
dates to around 1910,
has two emerald drop
pendants set in stag-
gered fashion, along
with an articulated
diamond collet and an
old European-cut
diamond bow.

The *Belle Epoque* era, which translated from the French means "Fine Period," refers to a time of settled and comfortable living that lasted from the end of the 19th century until the outbreak of World War I. As seen from this necklace, it produced an elaborate and sumptuous arts style.

Estimate: $35,000-42,000; *Magnificent Jewels, Geneva, May 18, 1995*

This Art Deco pendant necklace has been created from a 17th century Mughal emerald, suspended from an old mine-cut diamond geometric frame attached to a diamond spectacle link chain. The emerald, as was the style in India at that time, is richly engraved. This one has flowers on it, but other Mughal emeralds are covered in scrolling foliage and birds. Originally worn as pendants, they were often mounted as brooches once they had been exported to the West. This was partly to make them less susceptible to being knocked and partly to enhance their color, the theory being that more light can permeate a brooch. However, Chaumet, which created this necklace in about 1920, has kept its original form. The house of

Chaumet was originally founded in around 1780, by Etienne Nitot, in Paris's rue St Honoré, where it soon gained the patronage of the French court. It created the crown for the imperial coronation of Napoleon, a tiara as a gift for Pope Pius VII, and Empress Marie-Louise's wedding parure. The business then changed hands several times before 1874, when Joseph Chaumet joined forces with Prosper Morel, the then owner. After 11 years, Chaumet assumed complete control and the Maison Chaumet continued to create jewelry for the courts of Europe, Russia, the Near East, and India, much of it including distinctive floral designs that replicate nature.

Estimate: $50,000-65,000; *Magnificent Jewels, Geneva, May 16, 1991*

This 46 cm line necklace has a front section set with 11 graduated, rectangular-cut emeralds alternating with graduated diamond collet spacers that lead to a diamond collet necklace with rectangular-cut emerald clasp. A collet is a circular band of metal in which a gemstone is set. The total estimated weights of the emeralds and diamonds is approximately 48 and 55 carats, respectively. This necklace was the property of the socialite Vera Hue-Williams, who was born Vera Sklarevskia in Kiev at the turn of the century. She fled the Russian Revolution, along with her sister Olga and her mother Baroness Kostovesky in 1917, and ended up in Paris with few possessions but the jewels hidden in her clothes. At 17, the very beautiful Vera married an Englishman, who died ten years later. She married her second husband, Walter Sherwin Cottingham of the Lewis Berger Paint Company, in 1931. When he died five years later, she inherited his fortune and served as a director of Lewis Berger until selling her interests in the company in the 1960s. During World War II, Vera married Thomas Lilley, chairman of the shoe company Lilley & Skinner. With him, she founded the Woolton House Stud at their home in Woolton Hill near Newbury, England, and became a glamorous leading light in the horse racing world, winning the first running of

the King George VI and Queen Elizabeth Stakes with "Supreme Court" in 1951. Lilley died in 1959, and four years later Vera married — for the fourth and final time — Colonel Roger Hue-Williams, who died in 1987. Throughout her life, Vera traveled extensively, visiting friends, attending to her business interests, and holidaying in some of the world's most exclusive resorts. All these activities demanded glamorous clothes and expensive jewels. Vera's jewelry was usually of a very simple design, but always of the finest quality.

Estimate: $670,000-830,000; *Magnificent Jewels, Vera Hue-Williams, Geneva, May 18, 1995*

Some of the jewels in the sautoir below are believed to have been part of the collection owned by Empress Eugenie, the wife of Napoleon III. The gems were subsequently remodeled into this Art Deco piece which features emeralds, diamonds, and natural pearls. Composed of seven rows of pearls, each side of the sautoir has a matching emerald bead spacer and a diamond pierced cupola terminal, from which is suspended a single diamond collet and a large cabochon emerald drop. These two drops weigh approximately 54.01 and 50.72 carats respectively.

Estimate: $300,000-400,000; *Diamond and emerald jewelry sold on behalf of the late Mrs James D. de Rothschild, Geneva, November 16, 1989*

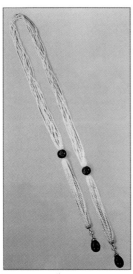

This stunning fringe necklace looks good enough to eat. From the double row of graduated cabochon emeralds and the pavé-set yellow diamond scroll with circular-cut diamond details hangs the drop-shaped, cabochon emerald fringe, from which the necklace takes its name. It was created by Verdura, a jewelry house set up by Fulco Santostefano della Cerda, Duke of Verdura, who moved from his native Palermo to Paris in 1926. Once there, he worked first as a

textile designer, and then as a jewelry designer, for the legendary Coco Chanel. Moving to the United States in 1937, he became a designer for the jeweler Paul Flato, before opening his own salon, on September 1, 1939, on Fifth Avenue. Verdura was inspired by the fanciful animals of his childhood and illustrations from his library. His jewelry featured gold mountings with precious and semi-precious stones — a bold undertaking at the time when platinum reigned supreme.

In 1972, Verdura sold his business and retired to London, where he lived until his death in 1978. The company still exists today, producing fine jewels from Verdura's original drawings in a manner consistent with his traditions.

Estimate: $30,000-38,000; *Magnificent Jewels, Geneva, November 21, 1996*

This Bulgari emerald bead and diamond necklace is quite similar in style to the bracelet seen on page 21, which is not surprising as they were both designed around 1930.

Two graduated emerald boule festoons with pavé-set diamond rondelle spacers and baguette-cut diamond stepped shoulders are suspended by an emerald boule, diamond rondelle, and pavé-set diamond lozenge neckchain, which is closed with a cabochon emerald and diamond clasp.

Estimate: $80,000-100,000; *Magnificent Jewels, Geneva, November 21, 1996*

This emerald and diamond pendant necklace has a front section of eight graduated, cut-cornered, rectangular-cut emeralds, each in a pear-shaped and circular-cut diamond surround, as well as an emerald pendant of similar design. The total weight of the emeralds is 169.85 carats and, according to the Gemmological Laboratory of the jeweler's, Gübelin, the emeralds are of Colombian origin. This is worth noting, because the geographical origin of a stone is important to its value, and Colombian emeralds are highly prized.

Gübelin, which was founded in 1854, has always been a family enterprise. Located in Lucerne, Switzerland, it was originally known for its superior quality watches and clocks. However, a collaboration with a New York jeweler, Edmond Frisch, led to the creation of jeweled watches and other fine jewelry.

Estimate: $33,000-42,000; *Magnificent Jewels, Geneva, November 15, 1995*

This unusual, but nonetheless very attractive, 58.5 cm long necklace is made from eight graduated emerald bead strands, which are held in place by several rose and old mine-cut diamond spacers of geometric design. The diamond line clasp is not quite visible in the picture.

Estimate: $42,000–$50,000; *Magnificent Jewels, Geneva, November 15, 1995*

This is another
interesting piece that
combines Eastern
gems with Western
design. The central
oval-shaped Mughal

emerald probably
dates from the 17th
century, as the front of
it is carved with the
lotus flower design
that was popular at

hexagonal cluster.
This, in turn, is
suspended from a
graduated three-row
pearl necklace that has
diamond buckle spac-
ers and a ruby and
diamond clasp.
However, the design
of this pendant neck-
lace dates only to
around 1925, when
Europe was obsessed
with the Orient.
This fascination,
sparked by the success
of Diaghilev's *Ballets
Russes*, was furthered
by Jacques Cartier (a
grandson of the
founder of the house
of Cartier), who
embarked on the
Polynesia at Marseilles
for his first journey to
India in 1911. On
returning to Europe
some years later,
having been greatly
inspired by the tradi-
tional Mughal carved
gemstones and the
colorful quality of
Indian enamel work,
he set about incorpo-
rating early Mughal
emeralds, cabochon
rubies, and carved
sapphires into his
jewelry. His work
then encouraged other
famous jewelers such
as Boucheron,
Chaumet, and
Mellerio to work with
Indian gemstones
carved in the shapes of
leaves, fruits, and
flowers.

that time. It is sur-
rounded by a diamond
and pearl palmette,
which is attached to a
cabochon ruby and
diamond shaped

Estimate: £50,000-
70,0000; *Jewellery,
London, June 22, 1994*

SUITES

Suite is the more modern name for a parure, a set of — for example — necklace, bracelet, brooch, and earrings, which are made of the same kind of gems and are designed to be worn all at the same time. Parures became fashionable towards the end of the 16th century and were revived in the 19th century. Traditionally, they are made with diamonds for formal wear and other precious stones for day wear.

Referred to as "a suite of emerald and 18 carat gold jewelry," this set could almost be a demi-parure as it consists of just two pieces — a necklace and a pair of earrings. The front section of the necklace, designed as a collet band, is made from tapered cabochons, which are unusual in that they are rectangular in shape — most are circular or oval. As mentioned previously, collet refers to the circular band of metal in which the emeralds are set, so a collet necklace is one in which gemstones set in a collet are linked together without any other ornamentation. The jewels, designed by the well-known French designer Pierre Sterlé, were sold in a red leather case embossed with the name of Chaumet, the firm to which Sterlé sold his business when in financial difficulty and to which he later returned as a consultant. The jewels come with French assay marks, which means that the gold has been tested to ascertain its purity.

Estimate: $25,000-33,000; *Magnificent Jewels, Geneva, May 18, 1995*

This suite of gem-set Cartier jewelry comprises a necklace, designed as a graduated carved emerald leaf band with circular-cut diamond, ruby, and sapphire spacers, a bracelet, and a ring; all mounted in 18 carat gold and all with French assay marks. Cartier, founded in Paris in 1847, by Louis-Francois Cartier, was creating jewelry for royalty shortly after its conception and has continued to produce top of the range goods ever since.

Estimate: $40,000-60,000; *Magnificent Jewels, Geneva, November 20, 1997*

This really impressive suite of cabochon emerald and diamond jewelry was created by Van Cleef & Arpels. The necklace, made from a cabochon emerald and circular-cut diamond cluster band, provides the base for a fringe of cabochon emerald and circular-cut diamond stylized palmettes. The suite also includes a bracelet and a pair of earrings, all of which are mounted in 18 carat gold and carry French assay marks.

The leading French jewelry house of Van Cleef & Arpels, which was founded in 1906, is famous for creating the *minaudière*, a sleek gold box with hidden compartments that was said to hold all the essential items for a well-dressed lady. In 1935, the firm revolutionized jewelry design by introducing the "invisible setting," when gemstones are mounted without any visible sign of a setting. In response to a more casual lifestyle, they also introduced a "Boutique" range in 1954, a concept which has subsequently been copied by other jewelers.

Estimate:
$200,000-250,000;
*Magnificent Jewels,
Geneva, November 20,
1997*

This suite of magnificent cabochon emerald and diamond jewelry may not look as impressive as the previous one, but its estimate was considerably higher. This suite has an extra component, a ring, and is mounted in platinum as well as gold, but it wasn't designed by a famous jewelry house, so the main reason for the higher estimate has to be the quality of the gems.

The suite comes with a certificate (no. 30829), dated October 6, 1997, from the SSEF Swiss Gemmological Institute stating that the emeralds in the necklace are of Colombian origin, accompanied by a note confirming the presence of a filler (identified as artificial resin) in the central emerald. As some of the most sought after emeralds in the world come from Colombia, the estimate on this suite was always bound to be higher than for the previous one. Emeralds, were used by the Indians in Colombia long before the Spanish arrived in 1538 and the world's finest emeralds have been found in the country's Muzo Mine.

Estimate:
$800,000-1,000,000;
*Magnificent Jewels,
Geneva, November 20,
1997*

The pieces of jewelry on these pages are not a suite, but are grouped together because they are three of the very individual works created by 20th century jeweler Sah Oved.

Oved developed her love of jewelry at art school in Chichester, England, but was largely self-taught. However, she did attend some evening classes during World War I and worked with John Paul Cooper, an Arts and Crafts designer, in 1923. Four years later, she started working with Moshe Oved, an eccentric Polish Jew who made watches and rings in the shape of new-born animals from his London shop. However, it was Moshe's religious beliefs that most influenced Oved. Born a Christian, she went to live in Jerusalem for ten years and returned to London imbued with Jewish traditions, which are strongly reflected in her work.

All of Oved's creations are one-off pieces, usually crafted from 22

carat gold. Her work is unique for its color, texture, and plasticity — it needs to be touched, as well as visually enjoyed — and many pieces are engraved with an inscription relevant to the theme of the jewel.

Today, her jewelry very rarely finds its way onto the market and, when it does, it is sought by collectors and museums, such as the V&A in London, for its unusual artistic qualities.

This is a unique, fully flexible emerald, ruby, and gold choker, which is made in sections, similar to Turkish amulet cases, each bearing an inscription in Cyrillic. The center section detaches to be worn as a pendant, and each plaque detaches to be worn with either a cabochon ruby and gold ring or a gold pendant attachment. It may also be shortened to be worn as a bracelet. The reverse of the choker is inscribed in Hebrew with Psalm 137 from the Old Testament and is dated 1934.

Estimate: $20,000-30,000; *Magnificent Jewels, New York, April 9, 1997*

This emerald, diamond, obsidian, gold, and silver slave bangle was designed as two sculpted gold kneeling figures, spaced by an emerald clasp, joined to a shaped silver and gold hoop. The two figures, with their heads on the ground, are in rapt adoration of God. Each side of the bangle is set with obsidian and rose-cut, near colorless, and circular-cut brown diamonds, bearing gold inscriptions in Hebrew. While one side reads "FROM THE HOUSE OF SLAVES," the other reads "TO BUILD UP ZION." Inspiration for this bangle almost certainly came from an old slave armlet.

Estimate: $8,000-12,000; *Magnificent Jewels, New York, April 9, 1997*

Oved used gemstones to impressive effect, as demonstrated by the sensational diamond, emerald bead, and gold necklace below. The diamonds are not faceted in the modern brilliant cut, but in a much earlier cutting style, confirming Oved's belief that her jewelry could look modern even when combined with more traditional elements. While each diamond is set into an individually shaped hexagonal gold mounting, the emeralds are set on truncated pyramidal mountings set at symmetrical intervals. As her jewelry was conceived like sculpture, it is possible to think of a piece of Oved jewelry as being a wearable work of art.

Estimate: $40,000-60,000; *Magnificent Jewels, New York, April 9, 1997*

The almost galactic-looking suite of emerald and diamond jewelry above, from Repossi, comprises a pair of ear clips and a twin-row emerald bead necklace with pavé-set diamond stylized quatrefoil spacers, focusing on a cabochon emerald pendant in a pavé-set diamond geometric surround. The jewelry business is in Alberto Repossi's blood. His father, Constantino, founded the family business in 1947, and Alberto began his career at the age of 18, when, accompanied by a cutter from his father's firm, he traveled the world in search of precious stones. In 1977, at the Hermitage in Monte Carlo, Alberto opened his own store, from where he has developed a reputation for artistic creativity.

Estimate: $72,000-88,000; *Magnificent Jewels, Geneva, November 21, 1996*

BROOCHES & BUCKLES

The brooch evolved from an ancient form of safety pin and has, over the years, been used to affix everything from garments, hats and turbans, to sleeves.

One side of this 1925 Art Deco lapel watch has a faceted emerald drop and an oval dial with black Arabic chapters, while the other has a carved emerald set in a circular-cut diamond surround. There are two types of lapel watch: those, like this one, which are suspended from a brooch and those which are attached to a stud that is inserted into a buttonhole. The former usually features a number of gemstones, but the latter tends to be quite plain. This particular watch is suspended from a circular-cut diamond and carved emerald chain, which is attached to a scroll platinum mount.

Estimate: $10,000-13,000; *Magnificent Jewels, Geneva, May 27, 1993*

Since World War II, the panther has become something of an emblem among Cartier jewels. The first clip brooches were made for the Duchess of Windsor in 1948, but the panther theme has since developed to include

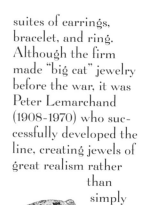

suites of earrings, bracelet, and ring. Although the firm made "big cat" jewelry before the war, it was Peter Lemarchand (1908-1970) who successfully developed the line, creating jewels of great realism rather than simply

stylized
forms. He
would spend
hours observing the
animals at Vincennes
Zoo and studying the
bronze cats of ancient
Egypt. The result was
extremely well mod-
eled miniatures, such
as this one, that
capture the grace and
authority of these
noble animals.
Made from diamond,
black onyx,
emerald, and
platinum, this
panther clip
brooch has a
rotating head, as
well as articulated
legs and a tail. It is
believed to date to
1970.

Estimate: $90,000-
110,000; *Magnificent
Jewels, Geneva,
November 20, 190⁻*

Brooches were very popular in the 19th century and, as a result, a great many were produced — in all styles, materials, and qualities. The settings were usually either gold or a combination of gold and silver, with the latter being used to show diamonds off to their best advantage. During Queen Victoria's reign, larger stones became very fashionable, reflecting the ornate decorative trends of the time. Typical designs incorporated elaborate scrollwork and complex foliate motifs, while settings — even though they appeared heavy — were generally hollow and lightweight. Turn a Victorian brooch over and you are likely to find a pressed-out, rather than a solid, back.

This Victorian lozenge brooch has a central, rectangular-cut emerald surrounded by geometric openwork of cushion-cut diamonds and diamond collet details.

Mounted in silver and gold, it is thought to have been made in around 1870.

In jewelry terms, a lozenge shape is a diamond figure with four equal sides, making two equal and opposite acute angles and two equal and

Another Victorian brooch, once again with a central, rectangular-cut emerald, but this time surrounded by diamond pierced openwork within an oval-shaped diamond frame with diamond collet detail. Of the same age, circa 1870, it is also mounted in silver and gold.

Estimate: $6,000-9,000; *Important Jewellery, London, December 1995*

Once the property of Baroness de Rothschild, these cluster brooches (created around 1860) each boast a square-cut Colombian emerald — one weighing 20.93 carats, the other 22.05 carats. Both the emeralds are known to have belonged to Queen Isabella II of Spain, who ascended the throne in 1833, at the age of two, and reigned until the age of 37. From the time that Spanish explorers first discovered Colombia in the 16th century, the Spanish royal treasury was never without a large number of high quality emeralds such as these.

The emeralds are both surrounded by an old mine-cut diamond cluster, with the total weight of the diamonds approaching 28 carats. The mounts are made from silver and gold.

Estimate:
$800,000-930,000;
*Magnificent Jewels,
Geneva, May 19, 1994*

From time to time, Christie's finds itself selling a gem or piece of jewelry for the second, or even third, time. For example, there is strong evidence to suggest that the diamonds and emeralds on this page and pages 66 and 67, were originally part of Empress Eugenie's jewels, which were sold by Christie's on June 24, 1872. The wife of Napoloen III, her jewels were without comparison among the European Royal families — with the possible exception of Russia. As a result, Empress Eugenie constantly out-dazzled the opposition at official ceremonies, great receptions, and court parties.

In the material distributed by Christie's prior to the sale in 1872, it was noted that the jewels being sold were remarkable not only for their diamonds, but also for their exceptional emeralds. Consequently, the Rothschild family purchased a number of the jewels, some of which were once again sold by Christie's in 1989.

This pendant brooch, with its square-cut emerald weighing 63.38 carats and its pearl frame with four diamond points suspending a pearl triple tassel, almost certainly belonged to Empress Eugenie.

Estimate:
$600,000-700,000; *Diamond and emerald jewelry sold on behalf of the late Mrs James D. de Rothschild's charitable trusts, Geneva, November 16, 1989*

These two pendant brooches also belonged to Empress Eugenie. The first has an old mine-cut diamond oval openwork mount and central rectangular-cut emerald weighing approximately 9.58 carats, which is further enhanced by four diamond collets at the cardinal points and a pear-shaped emerald drop weighing approximately 5.50 carats in a diamond surround. Mounted in silver and gold, it was made around 1860.

Estimate: $60,000-90,000; *Diamond and emerald jewelry sold on behalf of the late Mrs James D. de Rothschild's charitable trusts, Geneva, November 16, 1989*

The second has an oval cushion-shaped emerald (weighing approximately 17.47 carats), which is set in an old mine-cut diamond surround. Suspended from the main brooch is a single circular-cut diamond and a pear-shaped emerald drop weighing approximately 7.92 carats, with graduated old mine-cut diamond border. Once again, this brooch is mounted in silver and gold, and dates to roughly 1880.

Estimate: $350,000-500,000; *Diamond and emerald jewelry sold on behalf of the late Mrs James D. de Rothschild's charitable trusts, Geneva, November 16, 1989*

This large emerald and diamond brooch has an interesting provenance. In 1887, Marie, Duchess of Grafton, gave an emerald brooch and a pair of earrings (see page 80) to her grand-daughter, Marie Constance Mallet, who was maid of honor to Queen Victoria. In the late 1920s, the brooch was re-set and was passed on to the 1993 vendor by descent. Measuring 9.1 cm high, the central focus of the brooch is a square-cut emerald and diamond cluster, which is surrounded by a chased openwork scroll with an emerald outer border and diamond collet detail. With fittings to form two separate clips, it was presented in a fitted case with the retailer's address of Longman and Strongi'th'arm Limited, 13 Dover Street, London W1.

Estimate: £15,000–18,000; *Important Jewellery, London, June 18, 1993*

Not all
the wonderful
jewels sold by
Christie's cost
thousands. Made in
the style of a 19th
century animal
brooch, this emerald
and diamond ladybird
almost seems
affordable. The
brooch has hexagonal-
cut sapphire wings,
cabochon emerald and
diamond body,
cabochon emerald
eyes, and articulated
legs. It is just under
3 cm wide.

Estimate: $500-
$700; *Jewellery, Without
Reserve, London,
December 7, 1995*

Although this bird in a nest brooch is reminiscent of the animal brooches of the late 19th century, it was in fact created by Cartier around 1950. Made from 18 carat gold, the bird has engraved gold feathers, a cabochon emerald head, and a diamond and carved ruby tail. The nest, made from sapphire beads and gold wire, rests on a diamond and hammered gold branch.

Estimate: $8,700-10,500; *Important Jewels, San Moritz, February 23/4, 1996*

When this brooch came up for sale in 1996, it was considered to be the most important rectangular-cut emerald in combined value and size to come up for auction since the sale of Eugénie's emeralds in 1872. As a result, it is one of the most expensive ever sold. The rectangular-cut emerald weighing 47.76 carats is set within a collet-set old mine-cut diamond quatrefoil cluster. Made in the 19th century, it came with a certificate from the SSEF Swiss Gemmological Institute stating that the emerald is of Colombian origin. Perhaps not surprisingly, considering the size, color, and clarity of the emerald, this brooch has a very royal provenance — and it is not very often that stones from the crown jewels of one of Europe's main powers come onto the market. In its present setting, but as part of a necklace, this brooch was given by HRH the Duchess of Genoa, née Elizabeth of Saxony, wife of HRH Ferdinand of Savoy, Duke of Genoa, to her daughter when she married the Crown Prince, future King Umberto I of Italy, in 1868. It remained with Queen Margherita of Savoy-Genoa until her death in 1926.

Estimate:
$2,000,000-2,400,000;
Magnificent Jewels, Geneva, November 21, 1996

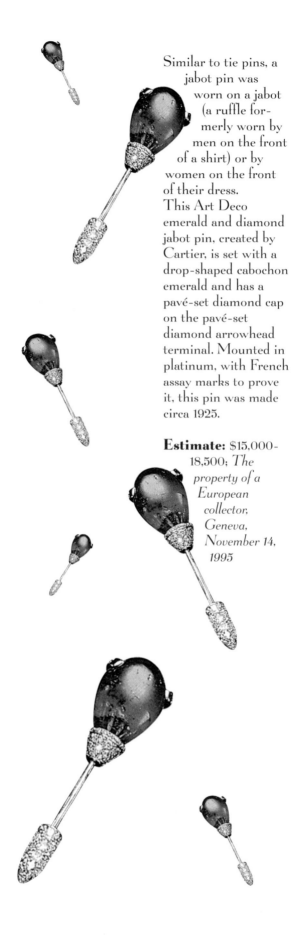

Similar to tie pins, a
jabot pin was
worn on a jabot
(a ruffle for-
merly worn by
men on the front
of a shirt) or by
women on the front
of their dress.
This Art Deco
emerald and diamond
jabot pin, created by
Cartier, is set with a
drop-shaped cabochon
emerald and has a
pavé-set diamond cap
on the pavé-set
diamond arrowhead
terminal. Mounted in
platinum, with French
assay marks to prove
it, this pin was made
circa 1925.

Estimate: $15,000-
18,500; *The
property of a
European
collector,
Geneva,
November 14,
1995*

This 10 cm long emerald and diamond brooch has a central emerald with pavé-set diamond petals and rose-cut collet diamond leaves and stem. Made circa 1880, it has Russian hallmarks.

Estimate: £2,800-3,200; *Jewellery, London, June 22, 1994*

When the price of a piece of jewelry isn't even listed in the Christie's catalog, you know it must be very expensive. This Art Deco emerald and diamond brooch, mounted with a rectangular-cut emerald of 142.20 carats, is such a piece. Created by Cartier, on the orders of the Aga Khan III in 1930, it was a family heirloom passed on to Sir Sultan Mohamed Shah Aga Khan III, who died in 1957 at the age of 79. He was the 48th Imam, as the political and spiritual leader of the Shia Imami Ismaili Muslims is known, which is a hereditary title that can be traced back to the Prophet Mohamed. Hence, the emerald is engraved with words from the *Qur'an* on one side and invocations of the divine names of God on the other — these divine names are recited during prayer or during mystical ceremonies; there are seven on the brooch. The inscriptions are characteristic of engraved gems from the 17th to the 19th century, produced in countries from Turkey to India. The particularly neat characters of the nasta'liq script in which the Arabic text is written, the lay-out of the script, as well as the type of cartouche used, suggest the engravings were made in Mughal India, during the reign of the Great Mughal Emperors in the 18th century. In 1739, Nadir Shah captured Delhi and his booty included what the French traveler Jean Baptiste Tavernier had admired in 1679: the "Darya-i-Noor" pink diamond, the "Koh-i-Noor" diamond, and many more treasures from the Mughal emperors. It is believed that the two emeralds left India at this time. They were then handed down through the Imperial Iranian family and given by Emperor Fath Ali Shah, who reigned from 1797 to 1834 and who established the collection of the Iranian Crown Jewels as we know it today, to his daughter Kurshid Kulah. She, in turn, left them to her daughter, Nawabalia Shams ul Molouk Lady Aly Shah, who bequeathed them to her son, His Late Royal Highness, Sir Sultan Mohamed Shah Aga Khan III. In recent years, the Iranian jewels were often handed over to Cartier to be given contemporary settings, hence the brooch's geometric border made of circular-cut diamonds and black onyx

No estimate:
Magnificent Jewels from the collection of His Late Royal Highness, Sir Sultan Mohamed Shah Aga Khan III, Geneva, May 12, 1988

These days, belt buckles are usually quite plain and simple, but that's not the way they started out. Some of the first buckles, made in Anglo-Saxon times, were really quite large and ornate, being made of gold and decorated with motifs and gems.

Throughout the late 6th and early 7th centuries, they were the main piece of male jewelry. This diamond, emerald, and ruby rectangular belt buckle harks back to those times. Measuring 8.4 cm wide, it was made by Boucheron, a leading French jewelry house,

in around 1920. It has a central diamond collet set within a circular-cut ruby and calibré-cut emerald design, with a leaf, scroll, and cluster border on a chased foliate ground.

Estimate: £15,000–£20,000; *Jewellery, London, June 22, 1994*

EARRINGS
EARRINGS

Earrings have been worn from earliest times, made from various kinds of metal, and in a wide variety of styles. However, their popularity really soared during the Renaissance along with a trend for shorter hair. They have been worn ever since, by both men and women.

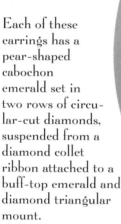

Each of these earrings has a pear-shaped cabochon emerald set in two rows of circular-cut diamonds, suspended from a diamond collet ribbon attached to a buff-top emerald and diamond triangular mount.

Estimate: $20,000-23,000; *Magnificent Jewels, Geneva, May 27, 1993*

These earrings feature a detachable pear-shaped cabochon emerald flexible drop in a circular-cut diamond spiked surround, which are suspended from a cabochon emerald and circular-cut diamond cluster mount.

Estimate: $30,000-35,000; *Magnificent Jewels, Geneva, May 27, 1993*

These are rather delicate Victorian emerald, diamond, and pearl earrings. They each have a cushion-cut diamond suspending a pearl drop within a diamond V-shaped enclosure to which is attached a rectangular-cut emerald and diamond cluster with a pearl fringe. Mounted in silver and gold, circa 1860, they come in a fitted case with the retailer's address of Longman and Strongi'th'arm Limited, 13 Dover Street, London W1.

Estimate: £2,500-3,000; *Important Jewellery, London, June 16, 1993*

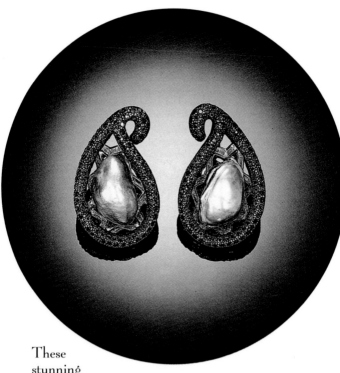

These stunning ear clips feature a baroque abalone pearl, surrounded by a zigzag of diamond openwork and a circular-cut emerald paisley-shaped frame. The mounts are made of all three precious metals: platinum, gold, and silver. Designed by Christopher Walling, the earrings were made at Carvin in France by master jeweler André Chervin. Walling was inspired to create them on a trip to Germany, during which he visited the Dresden Green Vaults and saw the channel-set and pavé-emerald "scales" on the dragon in Dinglinger's cup depicting Hercules and the Nemean lion. He had the emeralds set in silver with no underside mounting, so that, when held up to the light, they gave an effect similar to *plique à jour* enameling and used a pair of rare Venezuelan abalone pearls to provide an iridescence missing in most contemporary jewelry. The paisley shape was taken from Indian textiles and was a theme that Walling was to continue to use in subsequent pieces.

Estimate: $35,000-45,000; *Magnificent Jewels, New York, October 24, 1995*

TIARAS

This single-line band Victorian emerald and diamond tiara comprises a series of 17 graduated, square-shaped emeralds set within diamond entwined scrolls, which have been mounted in silver and gold.

Although it is English in origin, dating to circa 1850, it is very similar to an emerald and diamond tiara made by the Bapst, a German family who gained an enviable reputation for their

Tiara was the term used to describe the head-dresses of the ancient Persians. More recently, tiaras have been worn by female members of royal or noble families on state or formal occasions. Heavily encrusted with jewels, tiaras come in many different shapes and sizes, some of which can also be worn as necklaces.

jewelry in Paris over several generations. Their tiara, made in June 1820 for the restored Bourbon monarchy, was subsequently worn by Princess Eugenie. The similarity between the two pieces demonstrates the shared traditions of French and English jewelry during the first half of the 19th century.

Estimate: £120,000-150,000; *Magnificent Jewellery, London, June 20, 1990*

EMERALDS

This simple cabochon
emerald tiara has a
plain frame topped
with an angled row of
19 graduated cabochon
emerald drops, each of
which has a rose-cut
diamond cap. The
approximate total
weight of the emeralds
is quite considerable
at 209.38 carats.

Estimate: $480,000-
600,000; *Diamond
and emerald jewelry
sold on behalf of the late
Mrs James D. de
Rothschild's charitable
trusts, Geneva,
November 16, 1989*

The elegant, late 19th
century diamond and
emerald tiara
below has an
interesting
provenance.
Lady Rowena
Traherne inherit-
ed it from her mother,
for whom it was made
on the instructions of

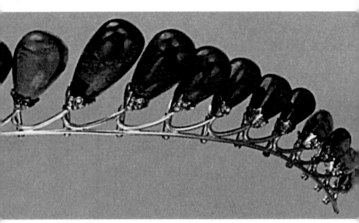

her father, the Marquis of Ailesbury. The Marquis was also the 10th Earl of Cardigan, a direct descendant of the 7th Earl of Cardigan who led the charge of the Light Brigade at Balaclava during the Crimean War.

The tiara is made of seven gradated cushion-cut diamond flowerheads with square-cut emerald and diamond cluster connections. The top flowerhead in the center of the tiara has an emerald and diamond quatrefoil cluster surmount. Note, too, the *fleur-de-lis* garlands close to the base of the tiara.

Estimate: $30,000-39,000; *Antique Jewels and Rings, London, October 9, 1996*

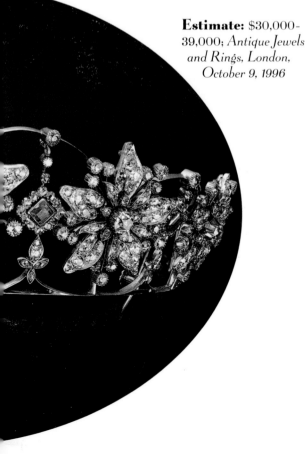

This *Belle Epoque* emerald and diamond tiara almost has a medieval look to it. However, it was made much more recently, around 1905, by Tiffany & Co, the leading American jewelry firm. Cabochon emeralds are set within a diamond openwork ribbon bow and garland frame.

Estimate: £18,000-20,000; *Jewellery, London, June 22, 1994*

Although considered an Art Deco piece, this tiara, made in 1923, by Cartier, pre-dates the *Exposition des Arts Decoratifs et Industriels* in Paris by two years. It is unusual in that it resembles a jewel-encrusted Alice band, rather than a traditional, horizontally placed tiara.

There are 19 fluted and engraved pear-shaped emeralds which alternate with pearl intermediary motifs, while the base has been created by graceful circular-cut diamond scrolls. The weight of the emeralds alone is 230.95 carats. The tiara once belonged to the Aga Khan III, whose wife, Princess Andrée, wore it on numerous state occasions, including the coronation of King George VI in May 1937, at Buckingham Palace.

No estimate: *Magnificent Jewels from the collection of His Late Royal Highness, Sir Sultan Mohamed Shah Aga Khan III, Geneva, May 12, 1988*

INDIAN JEWELS

The pieces of jewelry in the following pages were all created during the Mughal Empire, which lasted from 1526 until its gradual disintegration between 1658 and 1707, and the early days of British supremacy in India. Characteristic features of Muhgal jewelry include an extravagant use of gems, strings of pearls, pendants and tassles, and enamel work. Most of the pieces would have been made for members of the court and aristocracy, but cheaper pieces, made with gold or base metals and set with glass, were also produced. Mughal jewels were worn in rotation, so once they had been worn they were put away for 12 months until it was time for their next annual outing. All of them should be imagined in the setting in which they were worn: with jeweled brocade coats of honor, gold daggers, and ceremonial swords. Although the weight of so much clothing and jewelry must have been intolerable in the great heat of India, no Rajah would appear in public without it. Fully attired, he would stand out from the crowds, radiating reflected sunlight in all directions.

This late 17th century guluband has 11 large inverted, pear-shaped table-cut diamonds set in green enamel, which is fringed with diamonds, drop-shaped emeralds, and pearls.

The back of the guluband is as colorful as the front, having been enameled with the four colors then available to artisans: a glowing ruby red, considered the most beautiful by the cognoscenti, a brilliant translucent green, an opaque white, and a grayish blue. This enameling, known as *champlevé*, involved inserting enamel into gold hollowed out into the required pattern: in this instance, spiralling floral motifs. As an additional refinement, the hollows were hatched to increase the play of color as well as to ensure better adherence.

Estimate:
$85,000-110,000,
*Magnificent Jewels,
Geneva, May 16, 1991*

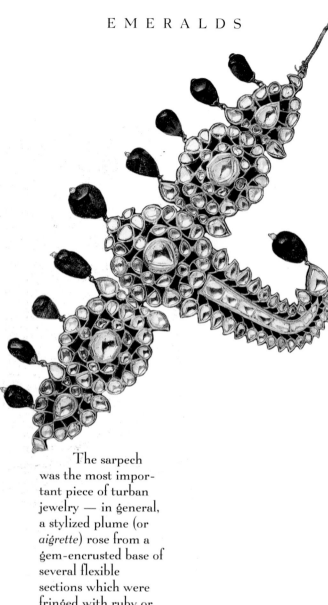

The sarpech was the most important piece of turban jewelry — in general, a stylized plume (or *aigrette*) rose from a gem-encrusted base of several flexible sections which were fringed with ruby or emerald drops. Some had a socket at the back to hold real osprey plumes or gold thread which would glitter in the sunshine. This 18th century sarpech has five flexible sections of open floral diamond panels suspending emerald drops, with an openwork tapering scroll plume and emerald bead pendant. Once again, the reverse is beautifully enameled in red, green, and blue bird panels, flanked by red, green, and white floral sprays.

Estimate: $85,000-110,000; *Magnificent Jewels, Geneva, May 16, 1991*

This 19th century
emerald, pearl, and
diamond forehead
ornament is composed
of a two-row pearl
and emerald bead line,
from which hangs a
circular diamond
cluster pendant with
a pearl surround, to
which are attached
five pearl tassles.

Estimate:
$8,500-11,000;
*Magnificent
Jewels,
Geneva,
May 16,
1991*

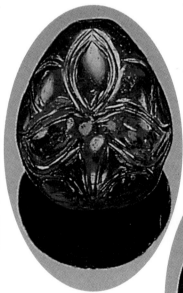

The pair of emeralds in these pendants were once owned by one of the premier families of India, whose ancestors were prime ministers during the Mughal Empire. The emperors often rewarded distinguished servants of the State for their exceptional services in high office with gifts of fine jewelry and it is possible that these gems were such a gift. One emerald weighs 42.61 carats, while the other is slightly larger at 56.33 carats. The emerald drops, carved with irises, were not necessarily earrings, they may have hung from a single necklace. If they were earrings, they may have belonged to a man, for men wore earrings in courtly circles from the reign of the Mughal Emperor Jahangir (1605-1625). Their earrings were usually composed of either a single pearl or — as in this case — emerald drops, which might be flanked by a couple of pearls. As far as a date is concerned, it is quite likely that these pendants were created in the 17th century, when the iris was commonly used in textiles and marginal illuminations.

Estimate: $400,000-450,000; *The property of a European collector, Geneva, November 14, 1995*

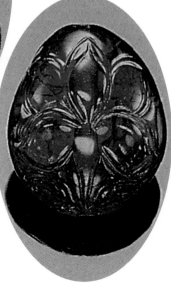

This
12.3 cm wide
belt buckle has a
central circular panel
designed as a carved
emerald, which is set
within a rose-cut
diamond, emerald,
and ruby border and
double
scroll open-
work panel
sides. It dates to the
19th century.

Estimate: £5,000-
£7,000; *Jewellery,
London, June 22, 1994*

Necklaces such as this one were created by goldsmiths who had their skills handed down to them through the generations. Without that indepth knowledge, anyone else would have found it nigh on impossible to produce this intricate emerald, diamond, and pearl pendant and necklace with repousse gold decoration on the reverse. And the emeralds, although they do not shine like modern gems, have a greater depth of color because they have been left in an uncut state.

Estimate: £35,000-40,000; *Jewellery, London, June 22, 1994*

E M E R A L D S

All photographs courtesy of © Christie's Images Limited 1999

INDEX